Dear Cheryl,

I'm so sorry for your loss. May you find some solace in the pages of this book. May my journey help you along in your journey!

Sincerely,
Jaynebelle Anderson

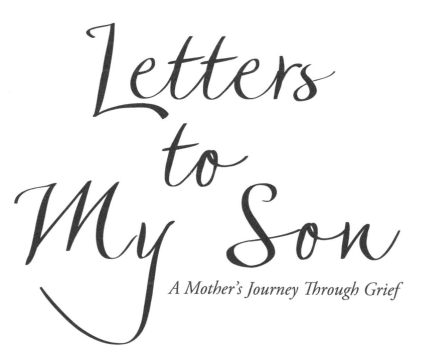

Letters to My Son

A Mother's Journey Through Grief

Daynabelle Anderson

ARCHWAY
PUBLISHING

Scripture taken from the KING JAMES VERSION: public domain.

This book is a work of non-fiction. Unless otherwise noted, the author
and the publisher make no explicit guarantees as to the accuracy of
the information contained in this book and in some cases, names of
people and places have been altered to protect their privacy.

Archway Publishing books may be ordered through booksellers or by contacting:

Archway Publishing
1663 Liberty Drive
Bloomington, IN 47403
www.archwaypublishing.com
1 (888) 242-5904

Because of the dynamic nature of the Internet, any web addresses or
links contained in this book may have changed since publication and
may no longer be valid. The views expressed in this work are solely those
of the author and do not necessarily reflect the views of the publisher,
and the publisher hereby disclaims any responsibility for them.

Any people depicted in stock imagery provided by Getty Images are
models, and such images are being used for illustrative purposes only.
Certain stock imagery © Getty Images.

ISBN: 978-1-4808-7277-6 (sc)
ISBN: 978-1-4808-7278-3 (hc)
ISBN: 978-1-4808-7276-9 (e)

Library of Congress Control Number: 2018914717

Print information available on the last page.

Archway Publishing rev. date: 12/21/2018

For my Jem
July 10, 1997–October 16, 2016

Acknowledgments

Thank you to my mom, Fanny, for raising me to believe I can do anything. Thank you to my husband, Eric, for the unfailing support you give me all day, every day. Thank you to my children, Matea, Ciena, and Sage, for making me laugh and giving me hope and strength every day. Because, at the end of the day, all you need is hope for good days and strength to live through the bad days for the good ones.

All my love.

Preface

The loss of a child breaks you. If you are lucky enough, you may be able to piece back most of who you were before the loss so that you are not a complete stranger even to yourself. Even then, you know that you will never be the same again. There will always be a piece of you missing. You are forever broken because of that missing piece.

And so, this is me. A forever-broken mom. Do I fight it and live my life trying in vain to be whole again only to punish myself over and over when my efforts result in failure? Or do I accept that this is me now? Do I allow and accept myself to be broken? And, most importantly, do I forgive myself for being broken?

I choose the latter. And this is my journey into that brokenness.

The Day

*I*t was like something straight out of the movies. It was a 3:00 a.m. phone call from your father that woke me. I didn't answer the first time because I was half asleep and wasn't sure what was happening. Then he called again. I answered, fully awake by then. He asked if you were home. I told him you were at F's house—that you had gone to a birthday party in Palos Verdes and spending the night at F's. He said he had gotten a call from someone claiming to be your friend. That friend said you were in a car accident, but he wasn't there, so he didn't know how you were doing. Naturally, I called M. She was sobbing when she picked up the phone, and I knew. I knew before she could even utter the words no mother should ever hear. I knew.

"He didn't make it."

And just as people do in the movies, I responded with, "Don't you say that to me! Don't you dare say that to me!" Looking back, I don't know why I said that. Maybe I watch too many movies. It just sounds so scripted.

Then more movie scenes … and multiple calls to different hospitals trying to find you. Multiple calls to the police station trying to get answers. My worst nightmare was now happening in real life: calling hospitals and police stations trying to find out where my only son was. We searched all the news outlets and online traffic reports.

Those two hours of trying to get a better answer than "he didn't make it" felt like an eternity. I spent many times in between phone calls down on my knees, begging God to not let it be true. To let M be mistaken. I promised to be a better person.

Then your dad got on a plane to come here from Las Vegas because he knew that this wasn't going to have a happy ending. Then I called your auntie Acel at 6:00 a.m. to come over and stay with your sleeping sisters.

Then came the forty-minute drive to the police station with Eric to get an answer since we couldn't get one over the phone. A sudden sense of peace came over me during that drive. I knew you were gone. And I knew I had to accept it. And I knew I had to be prepared to tell your sisters. Your nana. The world. But still, I waited for the director to yell, "Cut!" followed by "That's a wrap!"

But there was no director, because this wasn't a movie. It was my life. And I had to figure out quickly how to live this new life. How to live through this new life. How to keep my heart beating despite being shattered into a million tiny pieces. Then the police officer confirmed what M told me.

It was so surreal, sitting there in the impersonal lobby of the police station and being told by a stranger that my only son was gone. Everything else that followed was just one surreal event after the other. Stepping outside to call your *Ninang*[1] Wella to tell her (she was the first person I called). Driving to your nana's house to tell her in person and take her to our house. It was phone call after phone call. I repeatedly had to say, "Jem is gone."

Why did I do it? Make those painful phone calls myself? Maybe because I felt it was the right thing to do. Maybe because I secretly hoped that saying it over and over—"Jem is gone"—would help me become numb to this cold, hard truth and help me quickly accept this new fact of life, this new life.

---

[1] Tagalog for "godmother"

As you've said, I have to accept it simply because there's nothing I can do to change it. You are gone.

I love you,
Mom

Twenty-Four Hours After

J somehow made it through the first twenty-four hours. As an ER, ICU, and oncology nurse, I have seen death many times. I have seen the many ways loved ones handle the news of death. I have seen the different stages of grief. But I never realized that one could go through all five stages in fewer than twenty-four hours. In fact, I'm pretty sure I went through all five in the first six hours. First, there was anger upon hearing the words "he didn't make it." Then, there was denial, which was accompanied by hope that by the grace of God, M was wrong. Next came bargaining. I promised God that I would be a better person if he would just let M be wrong. Acceptance reared its head during that drive to the police station. Finally, I think depression has been intertwined with all the other stages, as I've had my bouts of sobbing in among all of these different emotions.

Needless to say, yesterday was exhausting. As the news of your death spread like wildfire, everyone came to our house. Your dad's family. My family. My friends. Those who couldn't come called. The house was packed. I remember thinking, *Jem would have loved this.* You were always such a social butterfly, talking to everyone. And afterward, you would have told me all sorts of stories about conversations you had with people. And not just half-assed stories but detailed ones.

I imagine your stories would have gone like this: "He said … then I said … then this happened and that happened." You always told stories the same way I did. As much as I seemed distracted (because sometimes the stories were really long), I truly enjoyed those times. It always made me feel good that my teenage son enjoyed talking to me. I remember the day you came for Ciena's birthday earlier this year. Your first night back, we stayed up past 2:00 a.m. just talking. You had a lot to tell me. I had to cut it short because I was getting so sleepy. Now I wish I had just let you keep talking. We probably would have kept going until the sun rose.

I hope you know how loved you were and still are. You touched so many lives and made such a difference in people's lives. When your dad and I got divorced, I often wondered if I would ever be enough for you. How could I be your mom and your dad at the same time? It wasn't that your dad wasn't involved, but since I had primary custody, I worried. Reading all the tributes about you made me realize that, somehow, I was enough. You grew up to be so amazing.

I love you,
Mom

Reality Creeps In

W hile October 16 will remain as the worst day ever, these past few days have been no picnic either. I suppose the upcoming days will also be rough. The coroner hasn't released your body yet. And since we hadn't seen you, "Is it really him?" still hung in the air. That was, until Eric and I went to the yard where they towed your truck. As your truck came into my line of vision, I was quickly transported to that dang movie set again. I saw myself fall on my knees as I let out a loud, "No!" and began sobbing. The truth was now staring me in the face. How your four passengers survived that crash is beyond me. But I am thankful that they did.

I remember saying to myself, "Get up!" As I walked around your truck to inspect the damage more closely, I wondered whether you were in pain or scared and whether you thought of me. I'm sure you thought of your sisters. My only solace is that maybe it happened so fast that there wasn't any time for you to feel the pain or even think that you were about to take your last breath. I hope so. I hope you saw Auntie right away. I hope she ushered you into heaven.

We collected all we could from the truck. And just when I thought my heart couldn't break into any more pieces, Eric pulled down the visor on the driver's side and found Ciena's picture in it. How many brothers carry a picture of their little sister in their car visors? You loved her so damn much that it makes the pain that much worse. Who will protect your sister now? She is going to take this so hard. She hasn't yet because she's been so busy with all the visitors. But once everybody goes back to their lives, Yaya[2] won't be there to comfort her. And that hurts me so much. When you left for Las Vegas, she couldn't stop thinking about you. How much more will she do so now?

Your dad retrieved your wallet and watch from the coroner's office; they wouldn't let him see you since there's no viewing room. In it, there was another picture of your Ciena, along with your newly acquired CPR card. You had just learned how to extract people from car accidents in your EMT class and save people's lives. Believe me—the irony is not lost on me.

But amid this storm, a ray of light came through. I finally got some answers. M came over. She told me everything. You and F were leaving the party after you found out another friend's mom had passed. So you were going to go comfort that friend. Then several other people tried to hitch a ride with you. But you accepted just three more passengers because your truck only had five seat belts (one for you, one for the front passenger, and three in the back). She told me how everybody was trying to pressure you into taking the other guy since he fit in the back with the others and didn't need a seat belt. But you stood your ground. Maybe you didn't like that other guy, and you just used the seat belt thing as an excuse. But whatever the reason, you saved his life! Then she told me you made everybody put on their seat belts, including F, who hates doing so. Four more lives saved.

You were wearing yours too, of course, but it wasn't enough to save your life. Life can be so cruel.

I love you,
Mom

---

[2] Ciena's version of "Kuya," Tagalog for older brother

Social Media

$\mathcal{S}$ leep has been elusive. Of course. I have found solace in your Instagram. I have looked at the pictures you've posted over and over. Read and reread your captions. Looked at other people's posts that you've liked and/or commented on. Same with your Facebook, but there isn't much there since you didn't really use it. I've even created a Twitter account just so I can follow you and read and reread your tweets. Online stalking at its finest.

I wish I could unlock your iPhone, iPad, and laptop, but we've tried every possible password with M's help, to no avail. Am I looking for anything in particular? No. I just want to read everything you've ever written, stare at every picture you've ever taken, and listen to every song on your very long playlist.

I've also taken comfort in reading your friends' posts about you on social media. So many wonderful tributes have been written. I can just imagine you coming to me, bragging about these posts. And then I would say something clever to try to bring you back down to earth. You would say, "Psshh." Then I would say, in all seriousness, "Of course they are saying these things. They love you."

Even though I have never met quite a few of them, I have reached out to say thank you for their beautiful words. They all responded, telling me I raised one heck of a son. To say that I am so proud to be your mom would be an understatement. One of your friends from Las Vegas replied to tell me that even though you made some amazing friends there, you missed me and your sisters so much, and that you looked up to Eric a lot. She then added not to doubt how much you cared for me and that you considered me one of your best friends.

Damn. Now what?

Mom

Is This Real Life?

$\mathcal{W}$ hen your body was finally released, it was officially time to make the final plans. I remembered making such plans for your auntie when she died. Uncle C and I visited two cemeteries, comparing the two as if shopping for land to build a house on. Then I went with him to pick out her coffin. Of course, it hurt then. After all, she was my only sister. And cancer sucks. But I did it for Uncle C so he didn't have to do those painful things alone.

Unfortunately, I have personally officially learned that making final plans for your child is painful beyond description. I was so dreading this part of the movie that when Auntie Acel asked me about going to a cemetery to check it out, I almost went along with it. Thankfully, Eric was paying attention and quickly reminded me that you wanted to be cremated. Everyone was shocked that we knew that. I get it. What healthy nineteen-year-old boy would tell his parents such a thing? I suppose one who has a nurse for a mom who talks about death openly and shares the problems that arise from not telling your loved ones your wishes before you die. I'm glad we had that conversation. I'm glad I get to honor your wishes.

But let me tell you—this sucks. I can't believe I am planning my son's final arrangements. How did I get here? How is this my life?

I love you,
Mom

Seven Days Post

A week ago, Eric and I received the devastating news from the sergeant that you were really gone. I am in disbelief that it's been a week since I last spoke to you. Since I last heard your voice. Since I last hugged you. Since I last said, "I love you." Since you last said, "I love you too." Since I last gave you money. Ha-ha!

I remember that last day so clearly. Eric and I had a conversation in the kitchen about how happy we were with you, your progress, and your growth since you returned to our home from Las Vegas. I hope that you were proud of yourself, too. Then in true Jeramie fashion, you woke up at noon and immediately proceeded to tell me all about your night at Magic Mountain while I put the laundry away. You even showed me a picture on your phone.

I miss you so much. The word *pain* doesn't even begin to describe how I feel. I've felt pain many times in my life: a broken ankle, giving birth, abdominal surgery, heartbreak, the loss of my grandparents times three, and the loss of my one and only sister to breast cancer. All were painful.

This is different. I've been describing it as dying a slow death. I just don't know how else to describe it. I keep thinking about our cancer patients who have said no more and go on comfort care. They must have this impending doom feeling like it can happen any minute; any second could be their last. I feel an impending doom

looming over me. An immense heaviness in my chest, wherein a full heart once resided.
I wouldn't wish this feeling on my worst enemy.

I love you,
Mom

A New Reality

I 'm sorry that you keep seeing me cry. I don't want you to be sad when you see that. I just really miss you. And I'm going to miss you forever. So, yes, I will be crying forever. Not as often as I do now, I imagine. But years from now, moments will continue to overtake me, and I will cry. That's just my reality now.

I love you,
Mom

Final Arrangements

*S*o many decisions to make. A part of me just wants to delegate them to others, but I know I must be the one to make them. I am, after all, your mother. You are my son. Were. Are. What is the correct way to say that? I will have to think about that some more later. I digress.

I decided to get memory cards printed to be handed to all who attend your celebration of life and memorial service, but I needed to decide which poem will go on the back. I really liked this excerpt from "The Broken Chain" by Ron Tranmer:

> You left us peaceful memories.
> Your love is still our guide.
> And though we cannot see you,
> you are always at our side.
>
> Our family chain is broken
> and nothing seems the same,
> but as God calls us one by one
> the chain will link again.

I like its hopeful tone and hope that we will see each other again. And we will be a whole family again. Someday.

I chose this poem by Genie Graveline instead. I think it perfectly captures who you are: someone who is always thinking of others. You would be comforting everybody through these trying times.

> Remember me with smiles not tears
> for all the joy through all the years.
> Recall the closeness that was ours,
> a love as sweet as fragrant flowers.
> Don't dwell on thoughts that cause you pain,
> we'll see each other once again.
> I am at peace try to believe,
> it was my time I had to leave.
> But what a view I have from here,
> I see your face, I feel you near.
> I follow you throughout the day,
> you're not alone along the way.
> And when God calls you, you will be
> right by my side right here with me.
> Till then, I'll wait by heaven's door,
> we'll be united evermore.

I hope I made the right decision.

I love you,
Mom

Borrowed Time

Auntie Acel asked me to write a poem for the back of the program of your memorial service. As I put pen to paper, I remembered how I wrote the poem for Auntie's memorial service program ten years ago. Then it struck me that I have to write your eulogy. This will be the third eulogy I have to deliver. I am not even in my fourth decade of life yet. First was your auntie's. Then Lola[3] Chong's three years ago. And now yours.

How did I get here? How is this my life?

Anyway, this is what flowed out of me. I hope you like it.

Borrowed Time

God loves me so
That he lent me you
To give me a glimpse
Of heaven, it's true
Nineteen years of bliss
With you, what a blessing
I gave you the world
You were my everything
In turn, you gave
Those around you your heart

---

[3] Tagalog for grandmother

Your kindness, your love
Made you stand apart
Alas, our borrowed time is up
God has called his son home
But in our hearts, you will forever be
Wherever we may roam.

I love you,
Mom

A Celebration of Life

*Y*our two-day celebration of life was beautiful. There were so many people. So many traveled from afar just to say their final goodbyes to you. Several of whom I hadn't seen in so long. A few I was shocked to see. It was always your nature to bring people together, and you are still doing it now—even in death.

The in memoriam video that Miles made is so heartbreaking and heartwarming at the same time. I have learned that I can feel pain and joy at the exact same time. So weird.

The stories everyone has shared about you have made me laugh and cry as well. I wanted to share stories about you, but how do I pick just two (one for each night)? I decided to go with the two stories that perfectly capture who you were as a human being and as a son.

The first story I shared was from your first two days in first grade. You came home after your first day and told me that a boy was mean to you. You asked him if you could play with him and his friends at lunchtime, but he said no. So, you just went and found someone else to play with. It took everything in me to not march to your class the next day and have a word with that boy. I decided to see how the rest of the first week went before I pulled you out of that school. Ha-ha!

I nervously awaited the news of how your second day went. You told me that the same boy was crying at lunchtime because his friends wouldn't play with him. When you offered to play with him instead, I knew you were going to be just fine. And I knew what a great big heart you had. Already so much compassion at such a young age.

The second story I shared was really about our mother-son relationship. I shared how much you loved talking to me about anything and everything. You rarely came out of your room while I was at work, but the second I got home, you would come out and start talking my ear off.

I also shared how when I was not home when you expected me to be home due to some plans that I didn't share with you, you would text me to find out where I was. It was a running joke with Eric and my friends whenever I was out with them. I would say, "Oh, there goes my teenager checking up on me." It was such an endearing thing. I loved it, and I am going to miss those texts so much. You were a mama's boy through and through.

I love you,
Mom

Eulogy

Alas, it was time for the eulogy. Someone asked if I was sure I wanted to do it: get up at the altar in front of everyone with your ashes in a box. I said, "Who else would do it? It can only be me." I didn't mean that no one else was welcome to do it. I just meant you would want it to be me. I think. I hope. Ha-ha!

What could I possibly say in such a short amount of time? I remembered something an old friend sent to me in the first few days of my grieving. It was a Bible verse, and I decided to use it as my guide. I kept it short and sweet since I didn't know how much of it I would be able to say coherently. I was prepared for the possibility of sobbing uncontrollably the whole time. Anyway, I hope I made you proud.

> As you all know, Jeramie was my firstborn. What you may not know is that he changed the trajectory of my life in a way that I could have never imagined. When I got pregnant with him, I was an art major because I had romanticized this idea of becoming a starving artist. But even though I was only a teenager at that time, I knew I had to change what I wanted to do with my life. During my pregnancy, I gave up TV for Lent and read voraciously instead. After reading an article in *Time* magazine about the children in Africa orphaned by the AIDS epidemic, I decided I wanted to do something that would

make a difference in people's lives. Little did I know then that already Jeramie's goodness was spreading to me as he grew inside my body.

And because he grew up to be a compassionate, polite, and loving young man, many were asking, "Why did this happen to him?" And while I grappled with this seemingly senseless tragedy, a friend sent me a story that brought some sense to it all. I would like to share that story with you all now in hopes that it will bring you some sense of peace, however minute.

Three ladies in Bible study came upon a verse in the Bible from Malachi 3:3, which said, "He will sit as a purifier and refiner of silver." Struck by this statement, one of the ladies decided to see a silversmith to figure out the meaning of the verse. After the silversmith explained to her the process of purifying and refining silver, the lady asked if he had to sit there and watch the entire process. He said yes because if the silver is left in the furnace even the slightest degree too long, the silver would become damaged. Before she left, she asked him one final question: "How do you know when the silver is ready?" He simply replied, "When I see my reflection in it." And so it is with God. He sits as our purifier and refiner. And when God and others see his image in us, we are ready to be removed from the furnace.

And so, Jeramie, in his short time on earth, with his pure heart, reflected the image of God and was ready to be removed from the furnace. And while I would like to take credit for raising such an amazing human being, he was born with a big heart, and it was he who changed me into the person I am today. Thank you, my son, for the indelible mark you have left on this world. You are my hero, my angel, my inspiration. I love you more than words can say.

Love,
Mom

Coroner's Report

*W*e finally received the coroner's report. When news of your death came out, I know everyone thought it was another tragic case of drunk driving. No one said it, but they didn't have to. I know they thought it. Perhaps they said it to each other—just not to me. Hell, I thought it (sorry!).

The police report was one of the first things we got right away, and your four passengers denied that you were drunk. I am aware that there was a possibility they were just trying to protect you. That even though you were gone, they still didn't want you to get in trouble. Teenage code.

When M told me the story of what happened that night, I knew you weren't drunk—but I still needed confirmation from the coroner's report. And I am happy that I got it. I am so proud of you. Even though you hadn't seen your high school friends in more than a year, you didn't get drunk with them and go behind the wheel. This was not another tragic case of drunk driving after all. This was just a tragic case. Period.

I love you,
Mom

Lost

Now that everyone has officially said goodbye to you, it is time for them to go back to their lives. But what does that mean for me? What do I go back to? Surely, there is no going back. Because going back would mean waking you up before I left for work so you could get ready for school. Going back would mean texting you and getting a reply. Going back would mean coming home from work and eating at the dinner table with no empty seat. But since none of those are possible scenarios, what do I go back to? If I can't go back to that life, where do I go?

I mean, where do broken hearts go?

I love you,
Mom

Your Things Are Not You

As the visitors have lessened, I have decided to start going through your stuff: your clothes, your shoes, your hats, your stuff. While I am definitely keeping some of them for myself, your sisters, and Nana, I've decided to reach out to your dad and closest friends to offer your stuff. Is it too soon? Nana thinks so. And I think your dad thinks so too, but I refuse to leave your room as some kind of sacred altar. Leave it untouched. As if you were coming back. But you are not coming back. I know that. I accept that. It is way more painful to pass by your room every day, with your door closed, because I know you are not on the other side of that door. I know that if I knock, your voice won't say, "Yeah?"

So, I'm cleaning it out. Not the furniture and the appliances. Just your stuff. I'm not trying to erase you from this house. That's impossible. Your pictures are everywhere. I just don't see the point of keeping your stuff in your closet. That feels like torture to me. And I'm already tortured. I don't need to add to my pain.

In talking to your closest friends, I made a funny discovery. One of them asked about your Yeezys. You were wearing them that night. I know that the coroner had to cut your clothes—so those were trashed—but I had completely forgotten to ask about your shoes. It turns out they were with you in the body bag. And you got cremated with your shoes. Your friend and I had a laugh about it.

Of course, you would get cremated with your Yeezys. That's exactly how you would have wanted it!

I love you,
Mom

Dream

I have to write this down fast before I forget. I dreamt about you for the first time. It's been more than a month since *the* day, and you finally came to me in my dreams. First, I was at the movies with several people. I think Eric was one of them. We came out of one theater, seemingly having just finished watching an Avengers movie. Then one of the people I was with said they were also playing *Captain America: Civil War.* We went to each theater, which had ten sections and no *Civil War.* The tenth theater was playing *Star Wars,* and I stopped there.

All of a sudden, the person I was with was you. I fell in line to buy you a ticket and a water. I gave you the water, and we went into a waiting room. You left me there with other parents, including an older Asian lady who was wearing a Palos Verdes sweatshirt.

After some time, I heard a piano playing. I decided to go look for you.

You were sitting on a bench looking out of the massive window into the city below. You had your Hulk book in your hand and were pretending to draw the city on the cover of the book. It looked like you were taking a mental picture.

I handed you the ticket and said, "I don't have any pockets. I don't want to lose it."

You took it from me, looked at your water bottle, and said, "You got this kind? This is a rip-off. You should email them."

I told you that it was okay and asked if you wanted anything else. You didn't say anything. Then I looked at the piano down the hall and saw that it was on auto-play. I made a joke and said, "Great recording." Still, you didn't say anything. I woke up.

My interpretation: The building/movie theater was all white, almost glowing. I think it was a waiting room to heaven. The room I was in may have been for parents who have all lost a child. The ticket was your ticket for entry into heaven, and you were just waiting for your time to go in. You were wearing a white T-shirt. You seemed sad.

And now I'm sad because you were sad in my dream. I hope you weren't sad in real life. But who am I kidding? I know you were hopelessly looking for a love like the kind that Auntie and Uncle C had. Even at your young age. And you had been devastated from not having found it. Maybe you were trying to fill a void. I don't know. But I hope you knew I love you and felt it. I love you so much.

I don't know what I'm supposed to do.

Love,
Mom

"Hey, Ya"

J heard "Hey, Ya" by Outkast on the radio today. I will forever associate that song with you. It made me smile remembering the time we were in my Honda Civic driving down Anza in Torrance on the way home to our apartment. You couldn't have been older than seven, yet you were already sitting in the front passenger seat—and without a booster at that! Wow, laws sure were different then. Although, in my defense, you were off the growth charts since you were so tall for your age.

When that song came on, we started singing and dancing. As we stopped at a red light, you looked over to the right. The people in the car next to us were smiling and watching us dance. You were so embarrassed! You slid down in your seat until they couldn't see you anymore, and then we went into complete hysterics! We couldn't stop laughing and laughed all the way to our apartment. The people in that car must have loved what they saw. I know I loved—and will continue to love—having that experience with you. Man, I miss that.

I love you. Don't be sad okay? We'll see each other again some-day, and it will be grand. We'll sing and dance to "Hey, Ya."

I love you,
Mom

A Series of Lasts

W hen a young person dies, it seems that the most common reaction is to feel saddened by the future that that young person is never going to have now that he or she has died. Many people certainly had that reaction to your death. People talked about how you were just a few days away from taking your EMT finals. Others talked about how you were planning to become an oncology surgeon because you really wanted to help cancer patients. Many people are sad that you did not get to live out that life.

While I am sad about those things as well, the biggest source of my sadness is the fact that I no longer get to make new memories with you. It's a very selfish reason, I know, but that is my truth.

In an attempt to hold on to as many memories with you as I possibly can, I have created a "series of lasts" on social media. Your Ninang Wella did a "series of firsts" when she lost her dad, but such a series seems sadder for me. I don't want to commemorate the first time I am doing anything without you, such as first Christmas, etc. Instead, I want to celebrate and relive my last memories of you and with you.

The series includes our last texts to each other, the last picture you took of me and your sisters, my last IG post you liked, the last time you checked up on me when I went out with my coworkers, the last thing you learned from your EMT class, the last time you commented on my IG, the last lessons we shared with each other, the last thing you asked for from the grocery store (ice cream, of course!), the last concert we went to (Foo Fighters!), the last thing I asked you to hang up for me in the house, our last trip to Disneyland, the last thing you posted on FB, your last birthday, our last family outing, your last IG post, the last time I congratulated you, the last gifts I gave you, our last family picture, and finally, your very last snap on Snapchat. Nineteen "lasts" for your nineteen years. I hope you like the series.

I love you,
Mom

Thirty Days Post

A month ago today, I went to bed not knowing that in a few short hours, my world would be shattered and my heart would be broken into a million tiny pieces. If I had known that that goodbye would be our last, would I have said something more? I told you that I love you. I would have said that, of course. And I hugged you. I would have hugged you as long as you would let me. I suppose I wouldn't have said, "See you tomorrow."

I would have told you that you are the best son I could have ever asked for. Yes, we fought, and we had our differences, but you are the true embodiment of why I prayed for a son when I was pregnant with you. I wanted my firstborn child to be a son who would love and cherish and protect his younger siblings, and that is exactly what I got! So, thank you for being the answer to my prayers. You have been such an amazing older brother to your siblings. Thank you for your unconditional love. Thank you for allowing me the opportunity to be your mom. Forgive me for any errors and mistakes I made in raising you—I was winging it most of the time as a teenage parent. Thank you for allowing me to grow up with you. Thank you for sharing your life with me.

Yes, that's what I would have said.

I love you,
Mom

Just Keep Swimming

My mood today:

> Grief is like the ocean: it comes in waves,
> Ebbing and flowing.
> Sometimes the water is calm,
> And sometimes it is overwhelming.
> All we can do is learn to swim.
> —Vicki Harrison

Maybe it's the lack of sleep, but the grief is overwhelming today. Good thing I know how to swim. Kind of.

I love you,
Mom

Gratitude

T hanksgiving. I was up all night. That is to be expected, right? We didn't always spend this holiday together, so I tried to imagine that you are simply spending it with your dad this year. I may be able to fool my mind, but there's no tricking my heart. The constant ache in my heart reminds me that you are no longer in this world.

I was up all night thinking about what I could possibly be thankful for in 2016. This year has been the worst year of my life. Then I remembered something a friend told me. She said that I feel great pain because the love you and I shared was great. And that's true. If I didn't love you, then the loss of you wouldn't really cause me much pain, if any. As odd as it may sound, I decided I am grateful for this pain because it means I have experienced one of the greatest loves in life. From this decision came this poem …

Gratitude

Despite the pain, agony, and sorrow,
I will give thanks on the morrow.
I will give thanks for the life we shared,
Grateful to have had you,
For whom I truly cared.
I am grateful to have been your mother,
Thankful to have had a son

Like no other.
Grateful for the nineteen years
I spent with you.
I will give thanks for our love,
So true.

    I love you,
    Mom

Ciena

*C*iena has been having nightmares. She doesn't remember them when she wakes up, but they are happening. Since October 16, we've let her move back into our bedroom. Eric, Ciena, Sage, and I have been co-sleeping. It's one big slumber party every night. Some party!

Anyway, she cries, kicks, and screams in her sleep (she usually screams, "No! No! No!"), followed by some serious sobbing. I don't wake her up from it. All I can do is hold her tightly in my arms and tell her I'm here and that I love her, tears streaming down my own face. Sometimes I sing "You Are My Sunshine." She eventually calms down and sleeps soundly for the rest of the night. She will start therapy soon. Her first appointment is coming up.

She has also had a few breakdowns during the day. Those days are particularly hard for me. My heart breaks even more when she cries and tells me that it's hard to live without you. Watching your five-year-old grieve brings a whole new level of pain and heartache.

Then I wonder how many times a heart can break before it's just broken permanently?

I love you,
Mom

Helpless

I 've been feeling so helpless as a mother. I am still so heartbroken over the loss of you, but my heart also aches for Ciena. She misses you so much. She just keeps saying that she wishes you didn't die. "Why did he have to die? Why did he have to leave me?" Impossible questions. Questions without answers.

I don't know why you had to die. Yes, I do believe it was your time. But I don't know why it was your time. Why your time came so soon. There was a car accident less than two miles from our house not too long ago. It was a Maserati. The front was completely wrecked. When I saw the pictures in the news, I thought there was no way the driver could have survived, but he did. He lives. A part of me thinks that's so unfair, but another part of me feels vindicated in some way. Like this confirms that it was, in fact, just your time to go. And there's nothing anyone could have done about it.

But how do you get a five-year-old to understand that—much less accept it? And this is the rare occasion when I find myself feeling angry with you. I get angry that you left her. How could you do this to her? Deep down, I know you didn't mean to. You would never intentionally hurt her. She was the love and the light in your life. Is. Was. Again, I don't know the right tense. Anyway, you would never leave her like this. Ever. I know that. I suppose I get angry because I feel defeated.

I don't know what to do.

I love you,
Mom

The Adventures of Yaya And Bubu Girl

*J*n an attempt to help Ciena with her grief, I've created a photo series just for her. *The Adventures of Yaya and Bubu Girl*[4] is a series of nineteen pictures of just the two of you accompanied by heartwarming stories. They have been posted on my social media, but I've also created a picture book for her so that she can read the book anytime she wants and look at the pictures. I hope knowing how loved she was brings her some comfort and that she can hold on to these memories of you forever.

Years from now, when she is a grown woman, I want her to look at this book and know that while her brother was good at many things, he was best at being a big brother. You embraced the role like no other. You took great pride in it. And while I miss so many things about you, I miss watching you be a big brother the most. I miss watching your sisters' faces light up when you enter the room and they say, "Yaya!" Then they would clamor for your attention, which made your face light up. I lived for those moments. The joys of motherhood. What I would do to have another moment like that again.

I love you,
Mom

---

[4] Jeramie's nickname for Ciena was Bubu Girl.

Because of You

So many things have happened in these last forty days. I find myself thinking, *Jem would love this.* That thought is quickly followed by another: *Oh, but this wouldn't be happening if he was still around.* Like everything we've done with Wowo⁵ so far, like celebrate his birthday. Obviously, he wouldn't be here from the Philippines if October 16 never happened. So, your death has brought people together. But would I rather have this than the other? Absolutely not. As much as I love my dad, his visit here is temporary. I would rather have you around for the rest of my life.

We still had Friendsgiving, and I kept thinking how much you would have loved hanging out with Dex. I miss you so much—like ridiculously so much. I feel like a different person now. I don't know if it's different in a good way or a bad way. It's just different.

I love you,
Mom

---

⁵ Jeramie's version of Lolo, Tagalog for grandfather

Perfectly Imperfect

J recently read an article in the *New York Times* written by Nora Wong. Her words struck me:

> The instinct to protect one's offspring runs through mothers of virtually all species. I violated the basic canon of motherhood. I failed to protect my child. That my child is dead while I still live defies the natural order.

When I wrote my eulogy, I wanted to say something similar to Nora's words. As a parent, my main job is to protect my kids from harm, and the fact that he is gone means I failed him.

I didn't include it because I know that as a parent, there is only so much I can do short of putting my children in bubble wrap and never letting them out of my sight. As a perfectly imperfect human being, I have to forgive myself—failure and all.

I love you,
Mom

Tattoo

W hen your auntie died, I got a massive tattoo on my back to commemorate her: a red sun with the words "Beautiful Day" written in Alibata, the ancient Filipino writing. I'm sure it was a surprise to no one that I got a tattoo to commemorate you. I got a replica of your first tattoo on my left ankle. I love the meaning behind your design: the lotus flower for inner strength and peace; Om for what was, what is, and what will be; and flames for the rage inside. It fits me so perfectly now as my past, present, and future bring about a constant rage that I must counter with my inner strength and peace.

Thank you for this gift. I hope you don't mind that I copied you.

I love you,
Mom

Back to Work

*T*he day has come. It's time for me to go back to work. It's not because I want to—it's because I need to. I have run out of paid time off. And since we can't afford for me to become a stay-at-home mom, back to work I go.

Eight weeks flew by. I'm sure people at work are not expecting me to come back. Like ever. Ha-ha! Was eight weeks enough? Enough for what exactly? To get over it? To feel better about things? To move on? No. No. And no. Infinity wouldn't be enough.

I wonder how people at work will act toward me. I am glad I work with compassionate health care personnel who are accustomed to death. There should be no weirdness or awkwardness, but I wonder if they will think I can snap at any given moment. I'd like to think I have mastered controlling my emotions and can wait to cry in private, but who knows? I suppose anything can happen. I need to be okay with crying in front of my staff and coworkers. I'm sure they'll forgive me.

I hope people aren't visibly uncomfortable when I see them. They might not know what to say to me or think they have to walk on eggshells around me. If they think I'm a fragile being who can break at any moment, I will feel bad for them. I will feel bad for making them uncomfortable. I will end up apologizing for making them uncomfortable, and I will try to make them feel better by reassuring them that I will be fine. That would leave me feeling sad and feeling bad for feeling sad. I don't want that. I don't want to feel bad for feeling sad. I just want to feel sad. I want people to be okay with that. I hope they accept the sad new me.

I love you,
Mom

Holidays

First Christmas without you here on earth. Somehow, I was able to find it in me to shop for loved ones. It was all online of course (thank you, Internet!). Since I know I can't just sleep through it because of your sisters, I wanted to still have you be a part of it. I hung your stocking with the rest of ours. I put goodies in it to be enjoyed by your sisters, and I bought a gift for you to be opened by your sisters. It was a remote-controlled flying toy. It's something I know you would actually like, but it's also something we can all enjoy in your absence. Watching your sisters open your gift was bittersweet.

In addition to the regular Christmas things we do, we also got a puppy. Ninang Wella's dog had a litter on Halloween; they didn't even know she was pregnant. Ha-ha! Anyway, we picked up our pup just before Christmas. Her name is Ms. Bea. She's a shih tzu. I know—I can't believe I got a small dog either! She's very cute and loving. I know she won't replace you; nothing ever will, but, at the very least, she will be another distraction for me, and a source of joy for your sisters, especially Ciena.

Besides wanting to sleep through Christmas, I also did not want 2017 to come. It will be the first year that you will not be spending a day on this earth. There will be no memories of you in 2017. There will be no memories with you starting in 2017.

I dreaded its arrival, but it came because I don't have the ability to stop time. I am doing my best to enjoy every new memory I make even though you are not here. I am doing my best to follow your lead and not just to live life, but to experience it. I hope I make you proud.

I love you,
Mom

Paralyzed

I must admit that I haven't been writing because I am paralyzed when I get the inkling to do it. I end up thinking, *What's the point? It's not going to bring you back.* I don't get to hear you respond. I have so much I want to say to you. I have so many questions to ask. I would love to connect with you—even just one last time.

I love you,
Mom

Moving Forward

P eople have given me the customary "how-to-deal-with-your-grief" books. Since I am such a bookworm, it must come as a surprise to you that I have been slow to read them. It's not because I am not interested. Partially, it's because I don't want to cry any more than I already do. I know reading some of these books will make me cry. I kept telling myself that I would start reading them when the time is right, but when I realized I didn't know when that time would be, I figured I might as well start sooner rather than later. So I did.

And I was right. I cried. Did I at least find comfort in knowing that I was not alone in my grief? Not really. I think because I have always known I am not alone in grief. I know many people who have lost loved ones. I have comforted many of them in my fifteen years as a nurse. When the sheriff broke the news to Eric and me at the police station, I wished it was a nurse telling me the news. It was not because he was rude or anything—because he wasn't—but he also wasn't comforting or warm. He was just a dude stating a fact.

The books were nice and well written, but I couldn't help but feel pressured to get on with my life, to move on, to feel better. What if I don't want to do any of those things? I mean, is there really a "getting over it" or a "moving on" or a "feeling better" from losing your child? I don't think so. I don't want to sound so negative, but the way I see it is I can't get over it simply because I don't want to. I guess I feel like getting over it would mean not missing you anymore. I want to miss you. Because I love you. You were literally a part of me. I gave you half of your chromosomes.

Maybe I do not understand the concept. That's quite possible. However, what I do know is that moving forward and moving on are two different concepts and that there is a moving forward from losing your child. I am doing that now. I have been moving forward since I woke up on day two after your death. I move forward every day. Every time I decide to get out of bed in the morning, I move forward. Every time I make breakfast for your sisters, I move forward.

People have asked me how I do it—this moving forward—and I tell them the truth. I do it by taking one step at a time and putting one foot in front of the other. When my eyes open to another day, I tell myself to get up. Once I get up, I tell myself to get your sisters ready for the day. After that, I tell myself to take a shower and get dressed. One. Foot. In. Front. Of. The. Other.

Every day that I choose life, I move forward. But the pain is ever so real. I live. I grieve. I am grief.

I love you,
Mom

Twitter

As I mentioned earlier, I created a Twitter account after your death so that I could follow you and read your tweets over and over. I wish I had followed you when you were alive. So many of your tweets are meaningful. I would have loved to discuss them with you. But since I missed out, all I can do now is find solace in them.

One of my favorites is the one you tweeted on November 1st, 2015: "Sometimes, even the worst endings aren't actually endings at all. I've learned, in my life, there is always another chapter to be told." I love it because you are so right. There is always another chapter to be told. I just wish the chapter had you in it.

I love you,
Mom

Politics

$\mathcal{J}$ don't know if you have been following what's been going on
here politically, or if you're even able to follow, but I really wish
I could talk to you about it all. I often think about this particular
tweet of yours: "If the opposite of con is pro, what is the opposite of
Congress? I love my country, but that shit's a mess." I would really
love to know what you would have to say about all of this.

All of this craziness has been quite a significant distraction for
me. I must admit, though, that I am not quite sure if it's a healthy
distraction. I mean, I teeter back and forth between being sad about
losing you and being angry about the current state of affairs; there
is no happy medium. One look at my social media, and I could see
how one would think I am certifiably insane. One day, I am post-
ing about you (sad, sad, sad) and the next day, it's all about politics
(mad, mad, mad).

I am quite sure that some of my friends and acquaintances are
somewhat worried about my mental health. Have I gone certifiably
insane? I don't think so. Is that denial talking? I really don't think so
either. The way I see it is this: I am still sad and still mourning the
death of my son, but I am also angry about what's happening in our
country. I am more than capable—and certainly allowed—to have
more than one powerful emotion at the same time. Even if October
16 never happened, I would still be angry, and I would still be just

as vocal about that anger. I have never been one to shy away from expressing my thoughts and opinions.

I think the idea that a person in mourning can't feel anything else is, frankly, quite foolish. Yes, a part of me died when you died, but I am not dead. Yes, sadness is now a big part of my life, but it is not the only part. So, yes, a sad heart can feel anger. A sad heart can feel joy. A sad heart can laugh, and not in that I-need-to-put-up-a-front kind of laugh, but in that I-am-genuinely-enjoying-this-moment kind of laugh.

Sometimes, that moment of happiness goes as quickly as it comes. It doesn't mean I am mentally unstable. It just means that I recognize that life is nothing but a series of fleeting moments. Sometimes, life goes as quickly as it comes.

I love you,
Mom

Alone

I know you know that I cry every day. I'm sorry. It's hard not to. I miss you so much. I'm overcome with grief. With sadness. With loneliness. But what did I expect, right? I am alone. In this. This grief is mine alone. Yes, there are many others grieving—everyone whose lives you've touched significantly—but their grief is theirs and this is mine. I am not saying mine is worse. In fact, it probably isn't.

I would even go so far as to say that my grief is probably not the hardest. Not because I loved you the least. That is utterly impossible. But because you and I ended on the best note possible. I know when we went our separate ways that night from the pumpkin festival at the Los Angeles Convention Center, that you had nothing but love for me, and I, of course, had nothing but love for you. I have no regrets. No guilt. No shoulda, woulda, coulda. I mean unless you count the "I shouldn't have let you go to the party" bit. But you and I both know that that would have never been a reality. That's just not how you and I rolled.

Anyway, a huge part of my sadness, especially these days, is I am one month away from half a year of not having you here. Six whole months. Seems unreal. But nothing about this seems real, I suppose. There's so much I should have written to you already, but I keep stopping myself. I am not really sure why. Maybe I am afraid that if I wrote it all on paper, this would actually all become real.

I don't know. Stupid, I suppose, but I am done stopping myself. I realize now that I have really harmed myself by doing that. I need to put my feelings and thoughts on paper.

I love you,
Mom

The Afterlife

As someone who has seen death on a regular basis, my thoughts on the afterlife have changed over time. I used to believe that after death, a person's soul goes to heaven to "live" happily ever after. Then it evolved to a belief in reincarnation. Then it became a combination of both. I believed that when a person dies, what happens to that person's soul depends on where that person was in Maslow's hierarchy of needs. Only those who have achieved full self-actualization go to heaven, and that heaven is not the same for every person. The rest are reincarnated, and the soul is given another chance to achieve full self-actualization.

Your death has rocked my thoughts on the afterlife. I am not really sure where I stand right now. Uncle C told me that when a person dies, the soul turns into energy. And that energy can sometimes manifest itself in ways that make you think of the person who died. Like when your iPad started playing a song when I was trying to unlock it. I don't know what song it was, but the lyrics kept saying "I'll take care of you." Or when I took a picture of Sage with my phone, but what showed up instead was a blob of purple "air" where her image should have been and the living room couch could still be seen in the background. Or when one of the four notifications I received today on Twitter was that "Jer followed amp."

I was at work when the notification came. I paused and thought it was odd. I checked your account to see if maybe you had been hacked. There was no new activity. So, I just figured it was a glitch and Twitter was delayed in notifying me who you were following. I went about my day.

As I tossed and turned in bed, sleep escaping me once again, that notification came to my mind. I decided to check amp's account. The picture didn't give away much. It was someone wearing a baseball cap, face partially covered, but I could tell it was a male. His bio didn't give away much either. So, I decided to read some of his tweets, hoping I would figure out who this person was. In the past twenty-four hours, amp had tweeted three times, each one with a very sad undertone. His last one in particular worried me. I decided to act. I sent him this private message:

> I can't tell from your picture if you're someone I already know, but I thought you should know that I got a weird notification from Twitter today telling me that Jer followed you on Twitter. Obviously weird because Jer is gone. So, I wasn't sure why I would get that notification now. Anyway, I saw your last three tweets, and now it makes sense. Jer wanted me to see those tweets and let you know that he is looking out for you. I hope you are okay and I'm sorry that you feel you can't make anyone happy. From my experience, we can't take care of others if we don't take care of ourselves first. So, take care of yourself, okay? Daynabelle (Jeramie's mom)

Imagine my surprise to find out it was A, one of your best friends from high school. I told him then that you came to me in a dream last month to tell me that the times you spent in the ocean with A last summer were some of the best times of your life. You also told me that A was still in great mourning. I know that I should have reached out to him then, but I didn't because I honestly feel like I should just leave your friends alone. After all, who wants to hear from their dead friend's mom? Anyway, I guess you were really pushing me to reach out to A. I'm glad that you managed to manifest your energy into a Twitter glitch. Even in death, you are still taking care of us.

I love you,
Mom

Numb

*J*n addition to the books, people who have lost loved ones have told me that you don't get over it—you just get used to it. You get so used to living with the pain that it seems like it hurts less. That makes sense. Eventually, people become numb to it. But until time affords me this perception of hurting less, I will continue to grin and bear it. Just bear with me, okay? Because the truth is, I miss you. All the time. Every second. Every hour. Every day.

I love you,
Mom

Before and After

My life has been divided into two distinct periods: *before* and *after*. Before you left this world. And after.

These two periods obviously are significantly different, but one of the main differences is found in the meaning of the word *okay*. It's such a simple word, and people may be inclined to think it cannot have a big difference in its meaning, but I beg to differ.

You see, in the period *before*, when one asked how I was doing, I had three standard responses, depending on my mood at that time: "I'm doing well. Thank you." "I'm good. You?" "I'm okay." The latter was usually reserved for times when I was a bit stressed or overwhelmed or upset or frustrated. The cause was usually related to work. As a nurse manager of two oncology units with more than one hundred employees, I found myself in that "I'm okay" mood every now and again.

Now in the period *after*. My only response to "How are you doing?" is "I'm okay." And of course, it's not for any of the same reasons I mentioned above. Oftentimes, I don't even know why I say I'm okay. Because am I okay? What does it even mean anymore? Okay by whose standards? Surely, I'm not okay based on my own old standards and meaning of the word, but I guess I say it because I am okay ... considering ...

I find that that's really what I want to say when people ask me how I'm doing. "I'm okay. Considering dot dot dot." But I don't want to make anyone feel bad or uncomfortable for asking. So, I stop at okay. But what does *okay* mean to me now? In this period *after*? It means I cry daily. Not the sobbing-uncontrollably-type of cry. It's more of the tears-just-start-streaming-down-my-face-all-of-a-sudden variety. The fact that I've accepted this as my new normal is why I say, "I'm okay." It is my way of letting you know that I am learning to live with my brokenness and that you shouldn't feel bad when I cry.

I love you,
Mom

Moana

A s much as I wanted to see this movie and take your sisters
to watch it, I didn't go rushing to the theater right away. In
fact, it took me a while before I could bring myself to watch it. All
because of the simple fact that you wanted to watch it. It was the
last movie you couldn't wait to see. When we were at the pumpkin
festival, there was a table by the exit with *Moana* merchandise, and I
vividly remember you saying to me, "I can't wait to see that movie."
Not something one would expect to hear from a nineteen-year-old
young man, but it didn't surprise me. That's how you were. You loved
the positive messages of Disney/Pixar movies. *Up* was your favorite
movie for some time, only to be replaced by *Inside Out*. The fact you
so openly embraced these movies made you so endearing.

Anyway, I hesitated to watch *Moana* because I felt like I would
be betraying you by watching it without you. You hated it when I did
certain things without you: concerts, movies you wanted to watch,
new restaurants, travel. You were even upset that I was going to New
York for the first time and not taking you. I mean, it was after all,
my honeymoon. Ha-ha! I promised that I would take you another
time. I'm sorry I never got the chance to do so.

Back to *Moana*. I finally watched it with your sisters. You would
have loved it. There was one line in the movie that I will carry with
me forever. As Moana's grandmother was about to take her last
breath, she said to Moana, "There is nowhere you could go where

I won't be with you." And it's so true. There is nowhere I could go where you won't be with me. And that brings me some comfort.

I love you,
Mom

My Plus-One

For several years of our life together, I was a single mom. You were my plus-one to many occasions from the time you were three years old. I took you everywhere with me. Weddings, lunches, or dinners with girlfriends. You never complained. And this was pre-smartphone and tablets. You were always just happy to go with the flow. Happy to go along with life.

As I lay wide awake again tonight, I want you to know that you inspire me every day. You lived life to the fullest. You loved fiercely. You were always *in* the moment. I will strive to be like that. Because as you tweeted on July 2, 2016, "People think about long term too much. Stop and do whatever makes you happy. Like, we can literally all die any second."

I miss you. I miss us.

I love you,
Mom

Your Day of Birth

*E*very sixteenth of the month is hard for me. That date has become a four-letter word. I can never sleep on the fifteenth because I dread the next day. It's as if I am expecting that phone call from your dad again. Holidays have also been hard, of course— Thanksgiving, Christmas, New Year's, your sisters' birthdays, Mother's Day—but your birthday has been extremely hard to face.

As I mentioned before, you and I didn't spend all the holidays together. Some years, you spent them with your dad. But your birthday has been the one special day that we never spent apart. Ever. Even during the years you were in Las Vegas for the summer. I made sure to go there and spend the day with you. Last year was no exception. I'm so incredibly glad we went there for the weekend to be with you on your birthday.

Now, here I am, without you on your birthday. I remember twenty years ago, on July 9, we went out to dinner for Nana's birthday. A few hours later, at 2:00 a.m. on July 10, I woke with a start. I was in labor. For the next several hours, I was in and out of bed, at times dancing around partially because I was so excited that you were finally coming—and because it helped with the pain.

Finally, just after 8:00 a.m., my contractions were close enough to head to the hospital. Fifteen hours of labor later, you entered the world and my heart. And now, twenty years later, although you are no longer in this world, you are still in my heart. And there you will stay forever. Happy twentieth birthday. While I mourn the amazing life you no longer get to live, I celebrate the wonderful young man you were.

I love you,
Mom

Seasons of Love

$\mathcal{J}$ remember the day I took you to see *Rent* (live, not the movie version). You were twelve years old. When some of the racier stuff and colorful dialogue were being performed on stage, I would cringe and think, *Maybe this was not the best idea I've had*. At the end of the night, I was glad I took you. It's a great story with very important life lessons. And now, when I think back to what an awesome human being you were, I am damn proud I raised you. So, yeah, pat on the back for me. And maybe taking you to these things and exposing you to different sources of positivity and light had an impact on your young mind.

And when I read and reread the beautiful messages your friends have left for you, I see why you didn't care that much about school. You had your mind set on offering the world one thing and one thing only: love. Loving is what you knew best and what you were best at. That's not to say you weren't smart—because you were—but you didn't want to offer the world your brain. You knew the world had plenty of brilliant minds already doing brilliant things. So, you offered your heart 'cause there's definitely not enough of that. Especially now, in this climate of hatred and violence, not enough people offering their hearts.

So even though you lived a very short nineteen years on this earth, what you did—the impact you made on people's lives in your short life—is immeasurable.

And so, I close this letter with lyrics from "Seasons of Love," one of my all-time favorite songs from *Rent*:

> Five hundred, twenty-five thousand, six hundred minutes. How do you measure a life of a woman or a man? In truths that she learned, or in times that he cried? In bridges he burned, or the way that she died? How about love? Measure in love. Seasons of love.

I love you,
Mom

Rumi

$\mathcal{I}$ saw this quote from Rumi the other day: "It's your road, and yours alone. Others may walk it with you, but no one can walk it for you." It perfectly captures the loneliness I've been feeling. The loneliness seems to have intensified in these past couple of months. As you know, I am all about analyzing feelings. So, the minute I noticed my loneliness had gotten worse, I began analyzing it. Why was I feeling lonelier than ever? This quote is why.

My pain. My grief. My sadness. My loneliness. All of it are mine. And mine alone. There are plenty of others in pain. Plenty are grieving the loss of you. Plenty are sad that you are no longer here. Many are lonely without your friendship and love, but we are alone in this journey of brokenness. Each one of us.

I've also come to realize that the loneliness has increased because as your one-year "angelversary" approaches—that's one full year of no new memories made with you. One full year of not hearing your voice. One full year of no texts received or sent. One full year of no hugs. One full year of no I love yous. And that hurts. Not as much as October 16 last year—but it's a pretty darn close second.

Anyway, I accept it. I accept the loneliness and the emptiness. I accept the pain and the grief. I accept this journey. Most of all, I accept the brokenness. But the acceptance doesn't make it hurt any less.

I love you,
Mom

One Year Post

J find myself in the same tragic movie again. One year without you. How can it be? One year without seeing you. One year without hearing your voice. One year without feeling your hug. One very surreal year. Twelve unbearable months, fifty-two excruciating weeks, 365 torturous days, 8,760 agonizing hours, 525,600 painful minutes, 31,536,000 heartbreaking seconds. It's unreal, but here I am.

Why won't this movie end? Is there a happy ending?

I love you,
Mom

Lanterns

For your twentieth birthday, I wanted to do something special. I know that's what you would have wanted. So, I invited friends and family to a celebration on the beach—one of your favorite places in the world. We had some of your favorite foods: sushi, spam musubi, and cake, of course. I also bought twenty floating lanterns. The plan was to light them up after sunset and release them over the ocean, but I didn't realize how windy it would be. So, I was only able to light and release one. And since that one blew toward the city, we didn't light the rest for fear of one landing in the brush and causing a brush fire. Disappointed, we went home with the remaining nineteen lanterns.

Determined to use them, we decided to go to Las Vegas on your one-year angelversary. We met up with your friends and family there (most of whom came down to LA for your birthday celebration). B had found a perfect spot in the Las Vegas desert, miles away from civilization. We all paired up and lit the lanterns. Although it was no easy feat, we were able to release several of the nineteen lanterns up into the sky. I hope they made it to you with our thoughts, our love, our everything. We miss you.

You are loved,
Mom

Forever Mourning

J was dreading your one-year angelversary last month. I was dreading it because I knew that every day after that day there would be no more, "A year ago today, we did this together." Instead, my most recent memories would be replaced with, "A year ago today, I was mourning the loss of my son." Every day hereafter. And here I am, one year and one month after, struck with grief. This night is a gentle reminder that I am forever broken. Lest I forget.

I love you,
Mom

Wind River

On our flight to Boston on Christmas, I watched *Wind River*. I didn't know anything about the movie. It had two actors from *The Avengers*, so I chose it as my in-flight movie. But now that I've watched it, maybe you willed me to watch it. It has a scene where Jeremy Renner's character, who had lost his daughter, is comforting his friend who just lost his. The dialogue hit so close to home and captured exactly what I have been trying to do with my grief:

> I got some good news, and I got some bad news. Bad news is you're never going to be the same. You're never going to be whole, not ever again. You lost your daughter. Nothing's ever going to replace that. Now the good news is, as soon as you accept that, and you let yourself suffer, you'll allow yourself to visit her in your mind, and you'll remember all the love she gave, all the joy she knew. Point is, you can't steer from the pain. If you do, you'll rob yourself, you'll rob yourself of every memory of her. Every last one, from her first step to her last smile. Kill them all. Just take the pain. You take it. It's the only way you'll keep her with you.

And so here I've been … just taking the pain. Trying to keep you with me. Every memory of you.

I love you,
Mom

How Many Children Do You Have?

*J*f there is one question that makes me uncomfortable, it's this one. I don't know how to answer it. Obviously, it used to have a clear-cut answer: four. Oddly enough, I don't know how to answer it now.

For some time after your passing, my answer remained four. But that question is typically followed by, "How old are they?"

I would usually respond, "Nineteen, twelve, seven, and two." Sometimes, when I am feeling a little bold, I say, "One was nineteen. The rest are twelve, seven, and two."

Nobody ever really reacted in any way that would let me know they caught the "was." Maybe they just thought I meant that one is now twenty, and I'm weird for saying "was nineteen." Ha-ha! Either way, the response would usually be either, "Wow! That's quite an age range," or "You have a nineteen-year-old?"

I suppose if I really wanted to hint further, I could say, "*Had* a nineteen-year-old." What would really be the point of that? I guess my trouble with the question is I don't want to mislead anyone by telling them I currently have four children. I mean, I guess technically I no longer have four children. Yes, you are my child. You will forever by my child. But I am no longer raising you. You are no longer taking up space in this world.

These new people I meet will never get the chance to meet you. So, lately, I have started answering the question with, "Three." Does that bother you or hurt you? I hope not. But as I write it down on paper now, I can see that it probably does bother you. I mean, why wouldn't I include you in the count? I don't have three children. I have four. There's no denying that. Maybe I can start answering with, "I had four children. But one is no longer with us." Just put it out there. The truth. Even if it makes the person who asked the question uncomfortable.

Yeah, I think that's how I'll answer from now on.

I love you,
Mom

Social Media Part II

$\mathcal{I}$ have a love-hate relationship with social media. I love it and hate it for the same exact reason: so much of what's on it reminds me of you. I regularly look at your social media because it makes me feel like I have interacted with you for the day. It's the same with seeing your pictures around the house. Nana has said that seeing your pictures makes her cry. It's the complete opposite for me. Seeing your pictures makes me smile, because I feel like I've seen you for the day. Is that weird?

I also look at your social media regularly because I like checking if any of your friends have posted anything new about you or have put up any new comment on your posts. Knowing that others are thinking about you—full of love and nostalgia—gives me comfort.

I hate it because when I see things that I know you would laugh at or find intriguing, all I want to do is tag you or send it to you. But I can't. Technically I can, but I won't get a response. We won't get to laugh about it together or have a discussion later. So, I end up doing nothing. I just get sad that I can't share these things with you. I am left to enjoy these little joys in life on my own.

I love you,
Mom

Call Me by Your Name

I stayed up all night reading *Call Me by Your Name* by André Aciman. I was completely enthralled by it. I felt compelled to finish it in one night. Why? What drew me in and captured me? Love is universal, and no matter what form it comes in, anyone can relate to a story about love. However, I knew something deeper was happening—even if I didn't know exactly what at the time.

As I was driving this morning, dropping off your sisters, one at school, the other at daycare, I figured out what that deep thing was. The story of loss drew me in and captured me. Love lost. It is universal and highly relatable.

The difference is my lost love is not of the romantic type as in the book. It's lost love period. Pure unconditional love. Happy love. Lost. Forever. And in the book, the two main characters are thrust into the "real" world—whatever that means—and have to deny themselves their one true love. Each other. They both go on living, but never whole, always a part of them missing. And in their brokenness, I found myself. I am Elio. I am Oliver. Never whole. Always a part of me missing.

I am fortunate enough to not have Elio's ending. He who lives his life as if he were in a coma, never truly moving forward and always waiting to be woken from his coma. Instead, mine looks more like Oliver's fate. He moves forward, but he never moves on.

He moves forward, living a parallel life to his what-could-have-been life with his wife and kids.

I am living a parallel life. This life after you. This life of never having you in it again. My love lost. My lost love.

I love you,
Mom

A New Life

$\mathcal{I}$ 'm exhausted. As an oncology nurse, I quickly learned that chronic physical pain causes fatigue, among many other things, but I never realized that chronic emotional pain causes the same. Until now.

These past two days, the exhaustion hit me like a train. It has rendered my mind utterly paralyzed. I can't move past it. I am overcome with sadness. Overcome with pain. Overcome with thoughts of you.

The exhaustion has created a new desire within me. A desire for a new life. A desire to start over. Start fresh. Start anew. Perhaps because if I were to live a new life, it would be perfectly okay that you are not in it. It is a new life after all. Some might say that I am already living a new life, but that is not entirely true. While this life certainly looks and feels different than the life I had prior to your death, it is not new. It is a life that has resulted from your death. There is a difference. In this life after you, I am reminded daily that you are not here to continue living this life with me. And that's exhausting.

So, I desire a new life. One without reminders. No, I do not wish to forget you. I could never forget you even if I tried. That much I know. Just a life that's new enough wherein doing something or going somewhere is not accompanied by a pang of sadness that you are not here to be a part of the experience. A life surrounded by people who never knew you and whose landscapes never had you in them, thereby affording me a landscape not ruled by the loss of you.

But I know such is not my fate. This is my life, and I have to accept it. And all the sorrow with which it comes—as broken as it is—I have to find a way to make the landscape more livable and less tiring to be in.

I don't know how yet, but I trust myself enough to know that I will figure it out. I have to.

I love you,
Mom

Music

Where words fail, music speaks.
—Hans Christian Andersen

L ike social media, I also have a love-hate relationship with music. I love it because it has been a significant part of my journey through my brokenness and grief. I have found such solace and comfort in so many songs. So many have been written about loss. Not necessarily loss of someone to death, but loss in general. I also love it because there are so many songs that remind me of you, of us. Like "our" song, "You'll Be in My Heart" by Phil Collins. When we saw Disney's *Tarzan* when you were just two years old, I started singing you that song as a lullaby.

When you got older, it remained our song. I remember clear as day, just a few months before October 16, you walked into my room while Alexa was playing it. You said, "Hey, our song!" My heart melted. You were nineteen years old, yet it remained our song.

My hate relationship stems from new music. Music that has since come out and that I know you would absolutely love! I can just see you and hear you getting so excited over the collaboration between The Weeknd and Kendrick, two artists you loved so much. When their song came out, I couldn't even believe it. I was legitimately mad. I felt that it was so unfair that they released it now. Like why couldn't they have done this before October 16, 2016? Why couldn't they have given you the opportunity to enjoy it?

It's a funny way to think, I know, but that is my truth. So, I did the only thing I could do: I became a fan of the song on your behalf. I listen to it every time it comes on the radio because I know that's what you would be doing. In this respect, I am partially living your life for you. I am enjoying things that I normally wouldn't enjoy just for you. As a sort of representative. I am representing you in life.

I love you,
Mom

The Loved Ones Who Get Left Behind

J remember a particular death in the Oncology ICU where I used to work. A young mother in her thirties had been battling cancer and had been in our unit for quite some time. She was fighting for her life—for her two young children. As it goes sometimes, the time eventually came when there was nothing more we could do for her except keep her comfortable. We had run out of lifesaving tricks. Her parents accepted this, and it was decided to let her go in peace. Free from cancer. Free from pain. Free from suffering.

When the moment came to take her off life support, her family gathered around the bed, surrounding her with love, along with us, her health care team, and the chaplain. Her children were crying and sobbing for her. "No, Mom, Mom, Mom!" They held on so tightly to her.

I started to sob myself, and I had to leave the room. I went straight to the bathroom to sob in private.

When I finally returned to the nurses' station—eyes puffy, nose running, trying hard to keep it together—another member of the health care team came up to me and told me that we did the right thing by letting her go. "Why are you crying?" she asked.

After the initial shock wore off from what I had just heard come out of her mouth, I informed her that I was not crying for the patient. I told her that I knew we did right by her and that she was now in a better place. Then I told her that I was crying for the family. I was crying for her mom who was silently crying at the foot of her bed, clearly dying inside but trying to be strong because now she had two young girls to raise. I was crying for her two young daughters who would have to grow up without the love and support of their mother. I told her that when our patients die, I always cry for the loved ones who get left behind because I am them and they are me.

I am them forever. We are united in grief.

I love you,
Mom

The Pause

Any time I say your name to someone who knew you and knew of the tragedy, there is always a pause in their breath. It's not significant, but I do notice it. Maybe it's a coincidence, but it happens every time. It's a sharp intake of breath, not immediately followed by an exhale. Almost like a tiny gasp. It's like the person is shocked by the sound of your name. Maybe they can't believe I speak so freely and nonchalantly about you. Or maybe they think I'm going to start crying at the mere mention of your name, and they are preparing themselves for the waterworks. Whatever the reason is, there's a pause.

Only a handful of people don't do it, and even fewer speak as freely and as nonchalantly about you as I do. I enjoy those conversations. I enjoy that there are others who are keeping your memory alive without the drama. It's no big deal—just two people speaking fondly of someone they love and adore.

I love you,
Mom

Take the Pain

A certain part of *Call Me by Your Name* really affected me. Toward the end, the father of one of the main characters talks to him about heartbreak and pain. The main character is heartbroken, and his father is giving him advice for how best to deal with that heartache:

> If there is pain, nurse it, and if there is a flame, don't snuff it out, don't be brutal with it. Withdrawal can be a terrible thing when it keeps us awake at night, and watching others forget us sooner than we'd want to be forgotten is no better. We rip out so much of ourselves to be cured of things faster than we should that we go bankrupt by the age of 30 and have less to offer each time we start with someone new. But to feel nothing so as not to feel anything—what a waste!

Much like the speech in *Wind River*, this speaks of taking the pain for all its glory. The advice he is giving his young son is to not be in such a rush to get rid of the pain. Doing so would require forgetting everything that has happened—not just the bad ending but all the good too.

I am not even trying to rid myself of the pain because I don't want to forget a single thing. I want to remember you every day and always. Forever. Even if it means I am reminded every day that you are no longer here. I will take the pain because I don't want to feel nothing to avoid feeling anything. I accept it, and I embrace it because I cherish my memories of you.

I love you,
Mom

Mother's Day

his was my second Mother's Day without you. I spent part of
the morning crying, of course, as I did last year. It's a harsh
reality to face, especially on days that are supposed to be about
family and happiness and togetherness. We went to Disneyland this
year. My decision. Sage has been asking to go every day for the past
week. So off we went. It was a nice day. Followed by an interesting
night and morning.

On our drive home, I immediately started getting the chills. I
thought I was coming down with a fever. The chills continued at
home. I was so cold that I had to sleep with a sweater and socks. I
even considered turning on the heater, but I knew everybody else
would get hot. Instead, I slept under a blanket and a comforter.

My sleep was interrupted several times in the first couple of
hours by Sage coming into the bedroom, only to turn around and
go back to her room.

In the morning, as I was brushing my teeth, Sage casually said,
"Yaya was here last night."

I tried to act cool so as not to alert her that what she said was
quite shocking. I replied with, "Oh really?"

She said, "Yeah. He looks like Tristan."

You do look like Tristan; he's just a skinnier version of you. I suppose that's what she meant when she said that you're skinnier now.

I asked her where she saw you.

She said, "Standing by my door."

I wanted to cry, but again, I kept it cool.

You are really something else. Thank you for visiting me on Mother's Day. I suppose that's why I was so cold. I wish I could have seen you. I'm glad Sage did. Come visit me again.

I love you,
Mom

Broken

*T*he exhaustion has rendered me useless. I literally did not want to get up from Auntie's La-Z-Boy for several days. I did of course, but as soon as I could get back in it, I did. I even slept in it at night. I usually reserved the nights for doing something productive, like running our two small businesses or writing to you. The nights are perfect for that because your sisters are asleep.

Instead, I have been useless. I could not find the energy to do any of those things. I took to watching movies. Every night, I would watch a movie or two until I fell asleep. Last night, I came across a movie called *Split*. I had not heard anything about the movie. When I read the brief description in the cable guide, I was reluctant to watch it because I thought it might be scary—and you know I am a wimp when it comes to scary stuff. So, I initially passed on it, telling myself that I would watch it another night with Eric. After browsing everything that was on or about to be on, nothing else caught my interest. Back to *Split* I went, and I decided to brave it and watch. Man, am I glad I did.

It's about how there's something infinitely special and unique and strong about people who are broken. After the movie, I was intrigued and researched what else I could find out about it. And what I found was very reaffirming of my belief about grief. In an interview in the *Hollywood Reporter*, M. Night Shyamalan, the master behind the film, stated:

This philosophy that the traumatic things, the things that have happened to us in our life, they definitely have changed us and changed people, but we tend to make it a pejorative, and say now you are broken. Now you are not whole. Now you are not like us. You are not normal. I'm not sure that's the case. Yes, they are different. And yes, we are different when something traumatic happens to us, but is it less now? Are we less? Or is the different possibly stronger? Is it something more?

I believe that being broken makes you stronger. It takes strength to be able to live—and to continue to live—a broken life. It takes strength to wake up broken, to face another day broken, to go through life broken. All of these things take strength, and that is why I accept my brokenness. I am not looking to fix it, get over it, or become whole again. On the contrary, I embrace my brokenness. I hope you do too.

I love you,
Mom

A Letter to My Readers

*H*ello. I am deeply sorry for your loss. I hope you can find some solace in my journey. I am writing this to address a very specific topic: mental health. Grief is tough. It can cause many mental health issues: depression, anxiety, substance abuse, and suicidal ideation, among others. If you are suffering from any of these, please seek professional help. Doing so does not make you weak. It makes you real. It makes you human. With that said, you may be wondering if I have seen a therapist for my grief. The answer is no. It's not because I don't believe in it. On the contrary, I believe therapy works—but your mind must be open to therapy for it to work.

When I was a teenager, I attempted suicide. I won't go into the details of that part of my life, but the attempt landed me in therapy. I had a psychologist, a psychiatrist, and the school counselor, but my mind was not open to getting help. I BS'd my way through my sessions, said what I thought they wanted me to say, not once opening up to what was really going on in my head and in my heart. Eventually, I didn't have to go anymore. Was I better? No. I remained a troubled youth. It wasn't until I got pregnant with my son that I straightened out.

Then my sister died. I had so much guilt. She and I had a tumultuous relationship. So, when she died, I felt I hadn't been the best sister I could have been. The guilt was worse than my grief. I decided to seek professional help. No BS this time. I was open and honest with my therapist. He discharged me from his care after six months. I felt better.

Why haven't I sought therapy this time? Because I have learned how to live with my grief. It doesn't overwhelm me. It doesn't keep me from living my life. It doesn't keep me from moving forward. However, the day after I wrote "A New Life," I did consider going to therapy because I was paralyzed. I was overwhelmed. But before I made an appointment, I decided to do something else first. For the first time since my son died, I shared my grief with my husband and a handful of my closest friends. I did this by sharing the link to my online journal, and they were able to read some of the things that are now in this book. And with that one simple act, I felt the weight lifted off my shoulders. Letting my loved ones in was my therapy. The paralysis was over. Broken as I may be, I continue to choose life. I continue to choose me.

Let me share one more thing with you. If you are having feelings of guilt, remember that guilt will not bring back your loved one. One thing you can do with guilt is use it as a driving force to be a better human to your loved ones who are still living. One of the things I felt guilty about after my sister died was not saying "I love you" to her. I mean, I did sometimes, but I didn't say it nearly enough throughout our relationship. So, I make it a point to tell my loved ones that I love them—every chance I get. It has become part of my everyday vernacular. I used that guilt to be the best mom I could be for my son. That guilt saved me from having any guilt now.

And if you're reading this not because you have lost a loved one but because you know someone who has lost a loved one and would like to know how you can help that person, my advice is to show up. Just show up. However you can. Show up by text, by phone call, by email, by mail, or show up at their door. Even after a year has passed—or two or ten—continue to show up. No matter how much time has passed, that person's loved one is still gone. A part of them is still missing.

All my love,
Daynabelle

Afterword

When I started writing these letters to my son, I never had any intention of sharing them with anyone—not even my husband. I wrote whenever the desire struck me. In fact, I wrote in three different notebooks and an online journal, which I used directly from my phone when I was stuck in bed with Ciena at night and couldn't turn on the light to write. I have always enjoyed writing. I was a diary-type of gal even well into my twenties. So, writing letters to my son was a very natural way for me to express my daily feelings and thoughts. And since I couldn't talk to him verbally anymore, I wrote to him. My main reason for writing was to speak to him in some way. Healing or recovery was never my intention, although writing has definitely helped me in my journey.

Why have I decided to share these letters now? You might be surprised. The decision came, in part, due to the Parkland students and the March for Our Lives movement. I bet you weren't expecting that answer, but bear with me. After the shooting at Marjory Stoneman Douglas High School in Parkland, Florida, I followed and supported the March for Our Lives movement.

And as I watched these brave young students—who not only survived a massacre but also lost many of their friends—I actually thought for one nanosecond, *Where are the parents of the victims? Why aren't they on the front lines spearheading this movement? Why are the kids left to try to protect themselves?* That thought was very quickly followed with, *I know exactly where they are. They are crying. Every day. In their son's or daughter's room. They are trying to figure out how to live this new life. New because their son or daughter is no longer in it. They are trying to make it through the day. And the next. And the next after that. They are here, where I am. In grief.*

That was the moment I decided to share my letters and share my journey. It's not because I think I am an expert on grief, but I want to help in some way. If I am able to help even just one person in their journey through grief, then my son won't have died in vain. My pain won't be for naught.

Thank you for taking the time to read this, and I am sorry for your loss.

Daynabelle

Bibliography

Call Me by Your Name. André Aciman. Atlantic Books, 2018.

Moana. Ron Clements, director. Disney.

Aaron Couch, "*Split*: M. Night Shyamalan Explains an Ending Years in the Making," *The Hollywood Reporter*, January 22, 2017.

Wind River, Sheridan, Taylor, director. Lionsgate.

"Loving My Son, After His Death." *New York Times*, Nora Wong. December 2, 2016.

Author and son on his seventh birthday at Disney World